READING

MAPS

Rolf Sandvold

Crabtree Publishing Company
www.crabtreebooks.com

Crabtree Publishing Company
www.crabtreebooks.com

Author: Rolf Sandvold
Coordinating editor: Chester Fisher
Series editor: Scholastic Ventures
Project editor: Robert Walker
Editor: Reagan Miller
Proofreaders: Molly Aloian, Crystal Sikkens
Production coordinator: Katherine Kantor
Prepress technicians: Katherine Kantor, Ken Wright
Project manager: Santosh Vasudevan (Q2AMEDIA)
Art direction: Rahul Dhiman (Q2AMEDIA)
Cover design: Sumit Charles (Q2AMEDIA)
Design: Dibakar Acharjee (Q2AMEDIA)
Photo research: Ekta Sharma (Q2AMEDIA)

Photographs:
Alamy: Danita Delimont: p. 18 (top)
BigStockPhoto: Pablo631: p. 23 (right)
Istockphoto: Jeremy Edwards: p. 5;
    Darshan Lakkur: p. 14 (bottom left);
    William Shane: p. 20; Mikhail Tolstoy:
    p. 4 (right); Maria Zhuravleva: p. 11 (right)
Jupiter Images: Comstock Images: p. 30
Map Resources: p. 17, 21, 25
Nationalatlas.gov: p. 12, 14 (top)
Photolibrary: Wolfgang Weinhaupl:
    cover (bottom right)
Pike Place Market PDA: p. 10, 11
Shutterstock: Elnur: cover (top left);
    Gabriel Moisa: cover (background);
    Denis Selivanov: cover (bottom left);
    Dwight Smith: p. 6; Aaron Whitney:
    p. 27 (center)
University of Texas Libraries: p. 1, 4 (left), 15
Visitseattle.org: p. 7, 9, 22, 23

Illustrations:
Q2AMedia

Library and Archives Canada Cataloguing in Publication

Sandvold, Rolf
      Reading maps / Rolf Sandvold.

(All over the map)
Includes index.
ISBN 978-0-7787-4270-8 (bound).--ISBN 978-0-7787-4275-3 (pbk.)

      1. Map reading--Juvenile literature. I. Title.
II. Series: All over the map (St. Catharines, Ont.)

GA130.S25 2008   j912.01'4   C2008-904949-7

Library of Congress Cataloging-in-Publication Data

Sandvold, Rolf.
      Reading maps / Rolf Sandvold.
          p. cm. -- (All over the map)
      Includes index.
      ISBN-13: 978-0-7787-4275-3 (pbk. : alk. paper)
      ISBN-10: 0-7787-4275-X (pbk. : alk. paper)
      ISBN-13: 978-0-7787-4270-8 (reinforced library binding : alk. paper)
      ISBN-10: 0-7787-4270-9 (reinforced library binding : alk. paper)
      1. Map reading--Juvenile literature. I. Title. II. Series.

      GA130.S27 2009
      912.01'4--dc22   2008033584

Crabtree Publishing Company

www.crabtreebooks.com   1-800-387-7650

Published in Canada
Crabtree Publishing
616 Welland Ave.
St. Catharines, Ontario
L2M 5V6

Published in the United States
Crabtree Publishing
PMB16A
350 Fifth Ave., Suite 3308
New York, NY 10118

Published in the United Kingdom
Crabtree Publishing
White Cross Mills
High Town, Lancaster
LA1 4XS

Published in Australia
Crabtree Publishing
386 Mt. Alexander Rd.
Ascot Vale (Melbourne)
VIC 3032

CONTENTS

Why Do We Need to Read Maps?   4

Different Kinds of Maps   8

Features on Maps   12

Symbols and Legends   16

Directions   20

Scale and Distance   26

What Do You Know About
Reading Maps?   30

Glossary and Index   32

Why Do We Need to Read Maps?

What is a **map**? A map shows an area and some of its features. You might use a map to find your way around a city. You could use a library map to find a special book. You might even use a map to find your favorite foods in a grocery store! A map can show a large area, such as a country or a continent. A map can show a small place, like your room.

▼ *Look at North America from space. It looks like the map!*

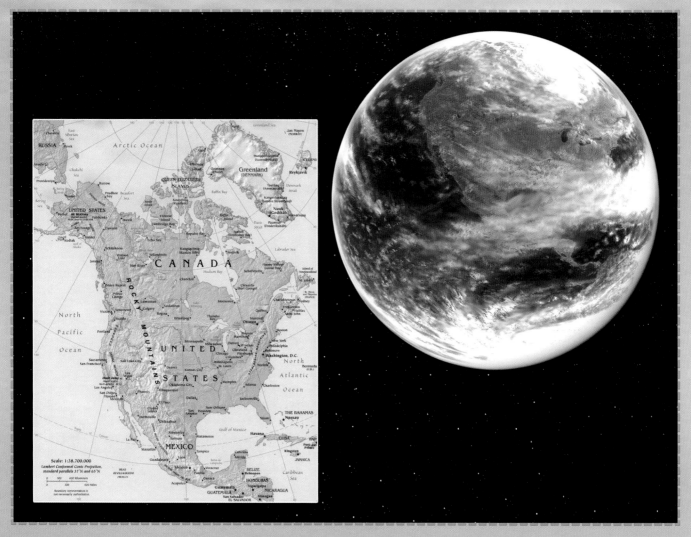

Maps can show the same place in different ways. That is because we use maps for different reasons. A map showing a playground at the park will look different than a street map of the same area. They have two different purposes. What maps do you know how to use?

*This is the Space Needle.
Can you find it on the map?*

This building is the Space Needle. We could see it in the photograph on page 5. This picture was taken close to the Space Needle. You can see more detail. How could you find this place if you visited Seattle? You could find it on a map!

A **symbol** is a picture that represents something. The Space Needle's symbol on the map is a circle.

The Space Needle is in the top left corner of this map. The map shows the streets around the Space Needle. It shows a few other things you might want to see.

▼ *The Space Needle looks different on a map!*

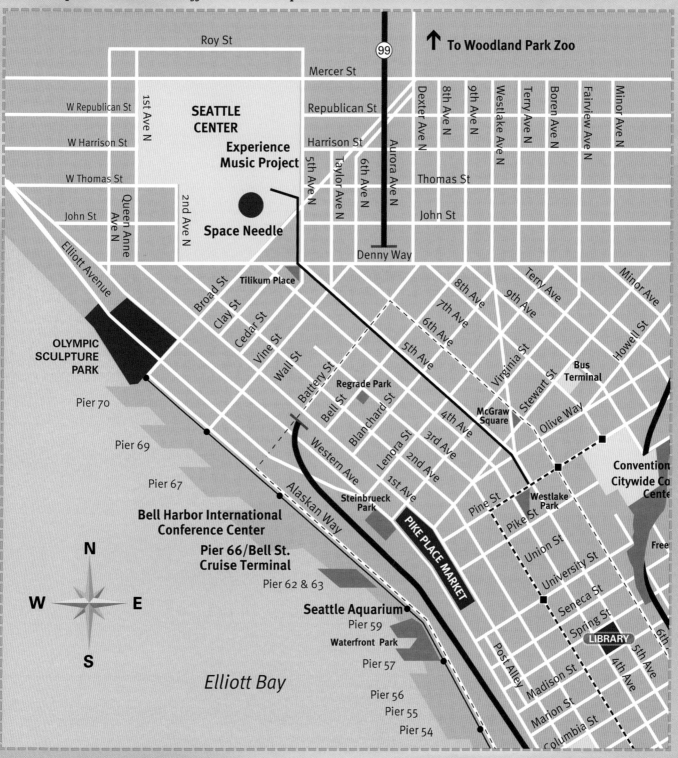

Different Kinds of Maps

We use different maps for different reasons. A map can show a country, a state, a city, or a part of a city. A map can help you get from one place to another. A map can even help you find your favorite roller coaster at an amusement park.

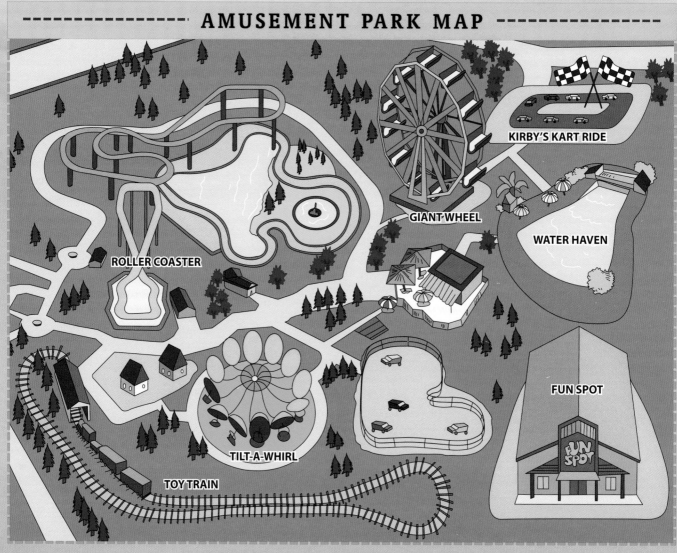

------------- AMUSEMENT PARK MAP -------------

KIRBY'S KART RIDE

GIANT WHEEL

WATER HAVEN

ROLLER COASTER

FUN SPOT

TILT-A-WHIRL

TOY TRAIN

▲ *Can you find the roller coaster on the amusement park map?*

Where you live, you might have a favorite place to play or meet your friends. A map would include the places that people would need to find it. In the map of the amusement park, you can find the roller coaster. In the street map of Seattle, a driver could find a street in town. The maps are very different. They both help you find places, though! If you drew a map of your favorite place to play, what would you need to show?

STREET MAP OF SEATTLE

Beaches
View Points
Shopping
Universities
Visitor Information
Major Parks
Scenic Roads
Major Roads
Freeways

Look at the map. What are some streets on the map?

Tourists in Seattle like to visit Pike Place Market. People at the market sell fresh fish, vegetables, fruit, and other tasty treats. Visitors would use a map like the one below to find their way around. This is another kind of map.

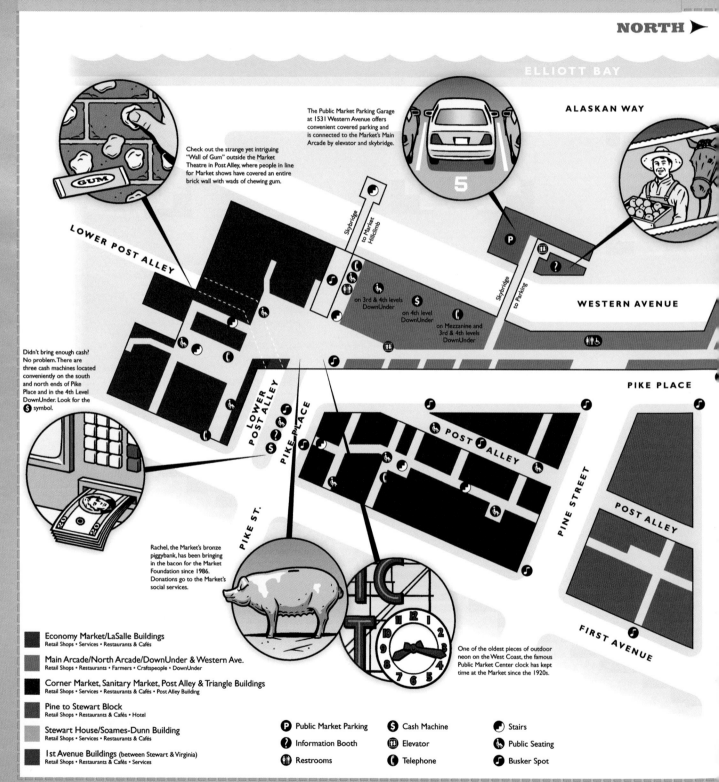

---------------- PIKE PLACE MARKET MAP ----------------

NORTH ➤

ELLIOTT BAY

ALASKAN WAY

The Public Market Parking Garage at 1531 Western Avenue offers convenient covered parking and is connected to the Market's Main Arcade by elevator and skybridge.

Check out the strange yet intriguing "Wall of Gum" outside the Market Theatre in Post Alley, where people in line for Market shows have covered an entire brick wall with wads of chewing gum.

GUM

LOWER POST ALLEY

Skybridge to Market Hillclimb

Skybridge to Parking

WESTERN AVENUE

on 3rd & 4th levels DownUnder

on 4th level DownUnder

on Mezzanine and 3rd & 4th levels DownUnder

Didn't bring enough cash? No problem. There are three cash machines located conveniently on the south and north ends of Pike Place and in the 4th Level DownUnder. Look for the $ symbol.

PIKE PLACE

LOWER POST ALLEY

PIKE PLACE

POST ALLEY

PINE STREET

POST ALLEY

PIKE ST.

FIRST AVENUE

Rachel, the Market's bronze piggybank, has been bringing in the bacon for the Market Foundation since 1986. Donations go to the Market's social services.

One of the oldest pieces of outdoor neon on the West Coast, the famous Public Market Center clock has kept time at the Market since the 1920s.

Economy Market/LaSalle Buildings
Retail Shops • Services • Restaurants & Cafés

Main Arcade/North Arcade/DownUnder & Western Ave.
Retail Shops • Restaurants • Farmers • Craftspeople • DownUnder

Corner Market, Sanitary Market, Post Alley & Triangle Buildings
Retail Shops • Services • Restaurants & Cafés • Post Alley Building

Pine to Stewart Block
Retail Shops • Restaurants & Cafés • Hotel

Stewart House/Soames-Dunn Building
Retail Shops • Services • Restaurants & Cafés

1st Avenue Buildings (between Stewart & Virginia)
Retail Shops • Restaurants & Cafés • Services

🅿 Public Market Parking $ Cash Machine   Stairs

❓ Information Booth   Elevator   Public Seating

Restrooms   Telephone   Busker Spot

A **globe** is a kind of map, too. It is round, not flat like the other map on the page. It shows the whole Earth. Remember that maps show where places are. A globe shows places all over Earth.

▼ *Look at all of the fun places to see at the Market!*

It would be hard to find Pike Place Market on a globe!

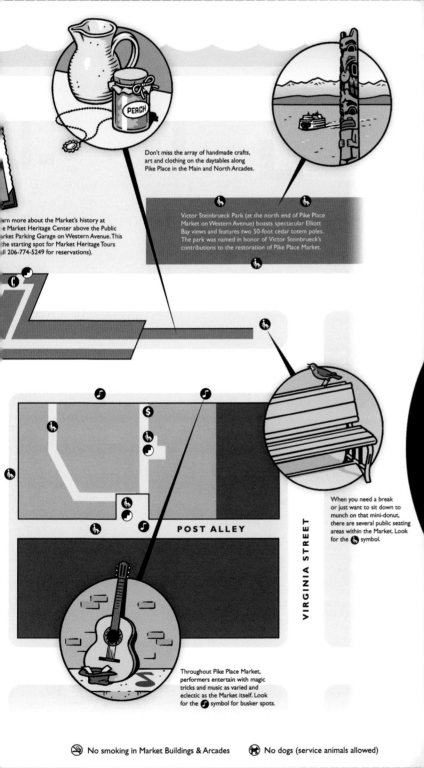

Don't miss the array of handmade crafts, art and clothing on the daytables along Pike Place in the Main and North Arcades.

Learn more about the Market's history at the Market Heritage Center above the Public Market Parking Garage on Western Avenue. This is the starting spot for Market Heritage Tours (call 206-774-5249 for reservations).

Victor Steinbrueck Park (at the north end of Pike Place Market on Western Avenue) boasts spectacular Elliott Bay views and features two 50-foot cedar totem poles. The park was named in honor of Victor Steinbrueck's contributions to the restoration of Pike Place Market.

POST ALLEY

VIRGINIA STREET

When you need a break or just want to sit down to munch on that mini-donut, there are several public seating areas within the Market. Look for the symbol.

Throughout Pike Place Market, performers entertain with magic tricks and music as varied and eclectic as the Market itself. Look for the ♪ symbol for busker spots.

No smoking in Market Buildings & Arcades   No dogs (service animals allowed)

Features on Maps

Maps can show different things. You have seen maps that show buildings like the Space Needle. Maps can also show things like rivers and forests. The things shown on maps are called features. People make some things featured on maps, like roads, cities, and buildings. The map of Pike Place Market showed many things made by people, like restaurants and stores.

▼ *The rivers and lakes on this map are all natural features. They are not made by people.*

Nature made other features shown on maps, such as mountains, rivers, and lakes. A globe shows natural features. Everything on the globe is made by nature. Many maps show both kinds of features. The map below shows natural features and human-made features. People made the train and its track. People made the streets. Nature made the land used for parks.

Map Facts

Many maps use color. This map shows the train's track in orange. A map that shows many bus routes might have a different color for each route.

The map below shows where the train travels.

The features on a map depend on what the map will be used for. The map below shows many cities in Washington State, including Seattle. Cities are human-made features. The map also shows parks, where people have saved the land for people to enjoy and for animals to use. The parks are natural features.

▼ *On the map, Mount Rainier is small. But look at the picture. Mount Rainier is huge!*

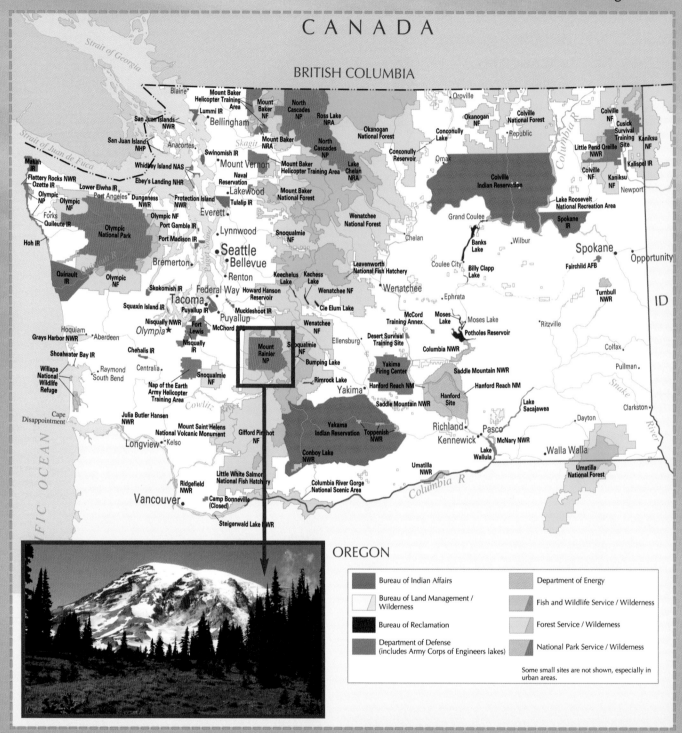

CANADA

BRITISH COLUMBIA

Strait of Georgia

Strait of Juan de Fuca

PACIFIC OCEAN

OREGON

Blaine
Mount Baker Helicopter Training Area
Lummi IR
San Juan Islands NWR
Bellingham
Mount Baker NF
North Cascades NP
Ross Lake NRA
Oroville
Okanogan Lake
Okanogan National Forest
Conconully Lake
Colville National Forest
Republic
Colville NF
Cusick Survival Training Site
Kaniksu NF
San Juan Island NHP
Anacortes
Skagit
Mount Baker NRA
North Cascades NP
Conconully Reservoir
Omak
Little Pend Oreille NWR
Swinomish IR
Mount Vernon
Mount Baker Helicopter Training Area
Lake Chelan NRA
Colville NF
Kaniksu NF
Kalispel IR
Whidbey Island NAS
Ebey's Landing NHR
Naval Reservation
Lakewood
Mount Baker National Forest
Colville Indian Reservation
Colville NF
Kaniksu NF
Newport
Makah IR
Flattery Rocks NWR
Ozette IR
Lower Elwha IR
Port Angeles
Dungeness NWR
Protection Island NWR
Tulalip IR
Everett
Wenatchee National Forest
Grand Coulee
Lake Roosevelt National Recreation Area
Spokane IR
Olympic NP
Olympic NF
Forks
Quileute IR
Olympic NF
Port Gamble IR
Port Madison IR
Lynnwood
Snoqualmie NF
Chelan
Banks Lake
Wilbur
Spokane
Opportunity
Hoh IR
Olympic National Park
Seattle
Bellevue
Coulee City
Billy Clapp Lake
Fairchild AFB
Quinault IR
Olympic NF
Bremerton
Renton
Keechelus Lake
Kachess Lake
Leavenworth National Fish Hatchery
Wenatchee
Ephrata
Turnbull NWR
ID
Skokomish IR
Federal Way
Howard Hanson Reservoir
Wenatchee NF
Squaxin Island IR
Tacoma
Puyallup IR
Muckleshoot IR
Cle Elum Lake
McCord Training Annex
Moses Lake
Moses Lake
Ritzville
Nisqually NWR
Fort Lewis
Puyallup
Wenatchee NF
Potholes Reservoir
Hoquiam
Grays Harbor NWR
Aberdeen
Olympia ★
McChord
Nisqually IR
Ellensburg
Desert Survival Training Site
Columbia NWR
Colfax
Shoalwater Bay IR
Chehalis IR
Mount Rainier NP
Snoqualmie NF
Saddle Mountain NWR
Pullman
Raymond
South Bend
Centralia
Bumping Lake
Yakima Firing Center
Snake River
Willapa National Wildlife Refuge
Nap of the Earth Army Helicopter Training Area
Snoqualmie NF
Rimrock Lake
Yakima
Hanford Reach NM
Hanford Reach NM
Hanford Site
Lake Sacajawea
Clarkston
Cape Disappointment
Cowlitz
Julia Butler Hansen NWR
Mount Saint Helens National Volcanic Monument
Gifford Pinchot NF
Yakama Indian Reservation
Toppenish NWR
Saddle Mountain NWR
Richland
Pasco
Dayton
Longview
Kelso
Conboy Lake NWR
Kennewick
Lake Wallula
McNary NWR
Walla Walla
Little White Salmon National Fish Hatchery
Columbia River Gorge National Scenic Area
Umatilla NWR
Umatilla National Forest
Ridgefield NWR
Vancouver
Camp Bonneville (Closed)
Columbia R
Steigerwald Lake NWR

Legend:
■ Bureau of Indian Affairs
□ Bureau of Land Management / Wilderness
■ Bureau of Reclamation
■ Department of Defense (includes Army Corps of Engineers lakes)
■ Department of Energy
■ Fish and Wildlife Service / Wilderness
■ Forest Service / Wilderness
■ National Park Service / Wilderness

Some small sites are not shown, especially in urban areas.

14

Now look at this map. It shows the hills, mountains, and hiking trails near Mount Rainier. What is a human-made feature? The trails are human-made. What is a natural feature? Mount Rainier is!

People made these trails for hikers to enjoy.

One of the biggest attractions in Seattle is the water! The map below shows Seattle and the water that surrounds it. Many tourists come to Seattle to see the water. How would these maps help them find their way? Let's pretend you are a tourist and find out!

First, you would need to get to Seattle. This map shows quite a few ways to get there. The legend shows you that there are interstate highways going to Seattle. An interstate is a road that travels through more than one state.

▲ A tourist would use the maps to find the way here.

MAP LEGEND

🛡 Interstate Highways

⬜ Bodies of Water

— Major roads

◀ Two interstate highways travel through this area. What is the symbol for an interstate?

This map shows me four marinas in Seattle. What is the symbol for a marina? Look at the legend to find out.

If you wanted to drive to Shilshole Bay Marina, what road would you take to get there?

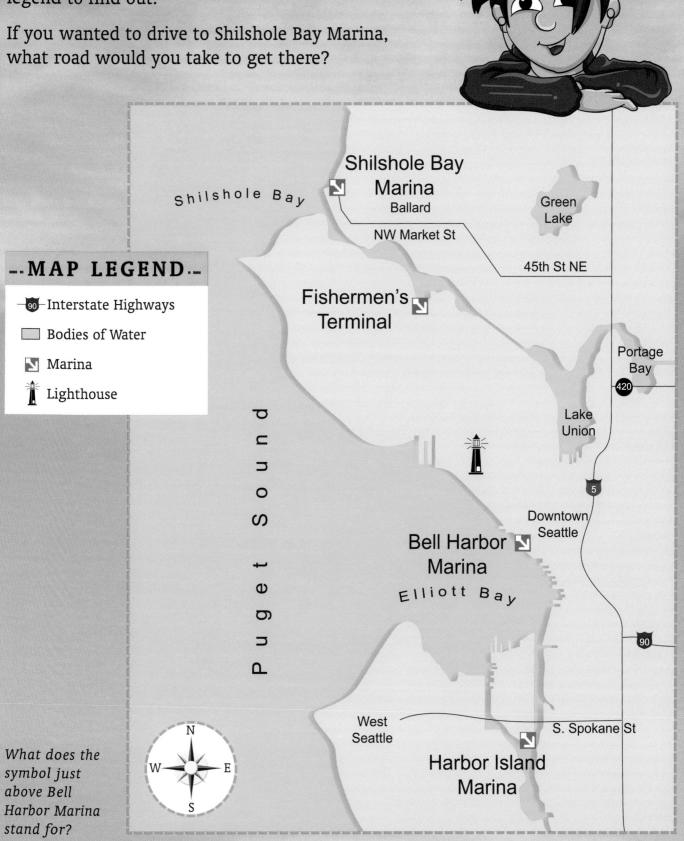

-- MAP LEGEND --

- Interstate Highways
- Bodies of Water
- Marina
- Lighthouse

Shilshole Bay

Shilshole Bay Marina
Ballard

Green Lake

NW Market St

45th St NE

Fishermen's Terminal

Portage Bay

420

Lake Union

Puget Sound

5

Downtown Seattle

Bell Harbor Marina

Elliott Bay

90

West Seattle

S. Spokane St

Harbor Island Marina

What does the symbol just above Bell Harbor Marina stand for?

Directions

Many maps have a symbol called a **compass rose**. A compass rose shows the directions on the map. The compass rose gets its name from a tool used to find directions, the compass. On a compass, the needle points "up" for north.

Does the compass rose look like a flower to you?

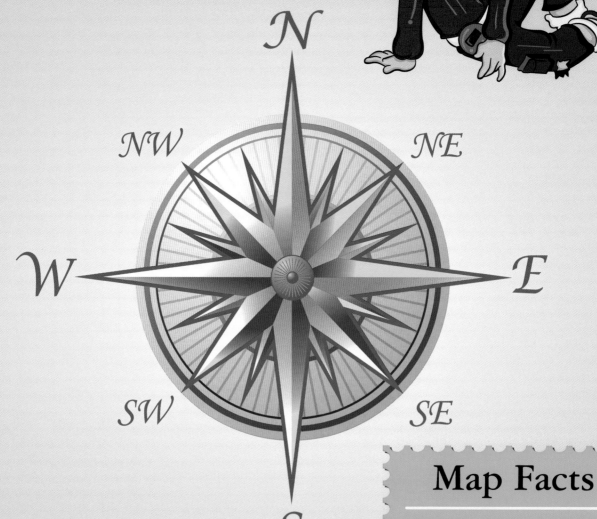

Map Facts

How can you remember the order of the directions around a compass rose: north, east, south, west? **N**ever **E**at **S**oggy **W**affles!

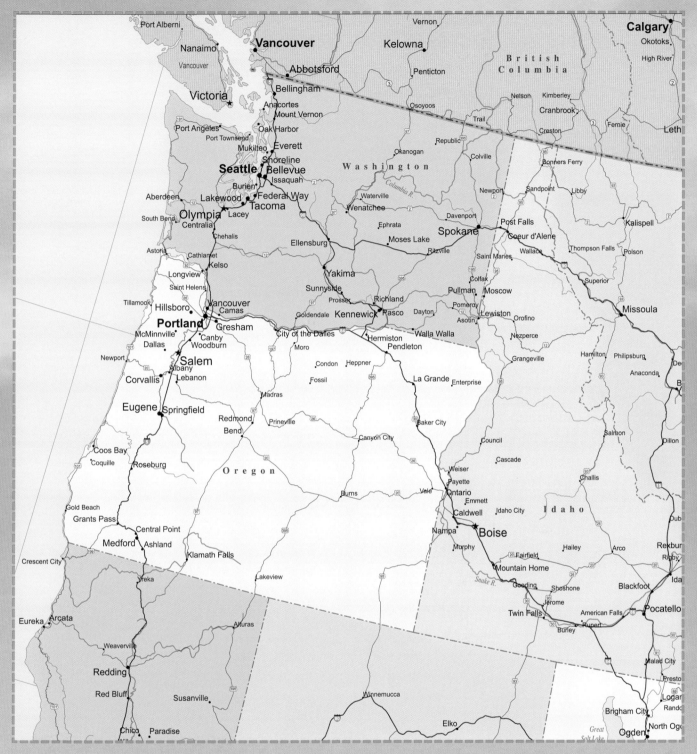

Most maps show the same direction at the top: north. The bottom of the map is south. The right side of a map is east, and the left side is west. You might go in a direction that is not exactly north or west but in the middle. That direction would be northwest.

Washington State is in the northwest U.S. Where is northwest on the compass rose?

You can use directions to describe the **relative locations** of features. Relative location is the location of something in relation to something else. For example, you could say that Seattle is close to Mount Rainier. You could say that Seattle is north of Portland. You would know approximately where you can find Mount Rainier and Portland.

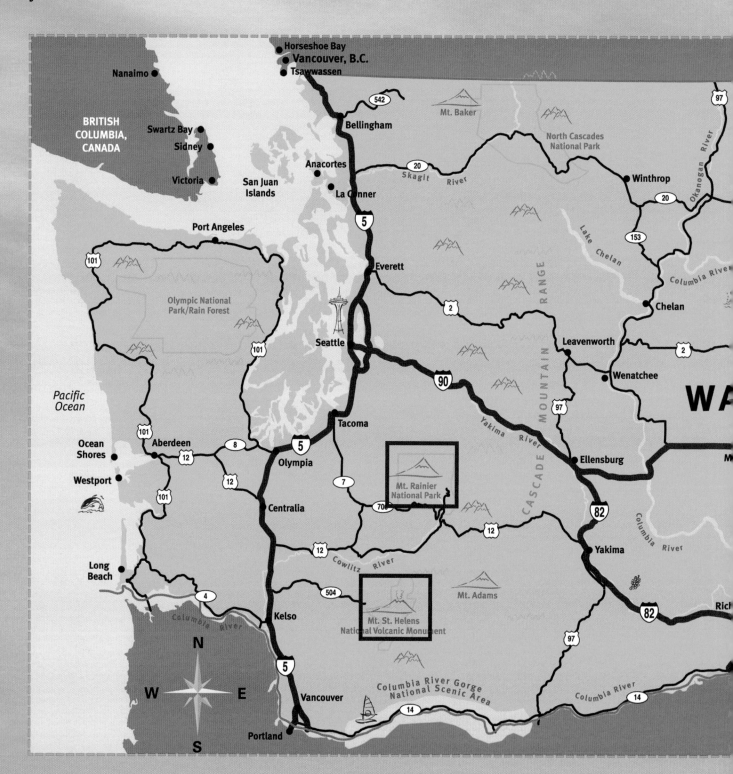

This map shows Mount Rainier and Mount Saint Helens. Both of these mountains are volcanoes. If you are going to travel from one of these mountains to the other, in which direction would you travel?

The abbreviation Mt. stands for Mount.

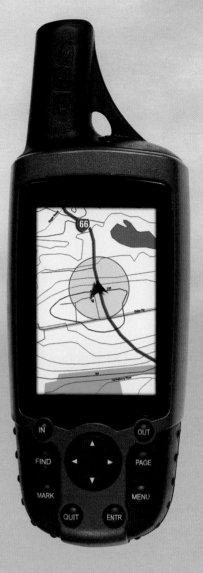

▲ *What city is close to Mount Rainier?*

Map Facts

A **Global Positioning System** (GPS) is a way to find directions. Machines in space find the location of a GPS and then send signals to Earth. The signals help people find their way.

Directions can help you find locations, but there is a more exact way to describe any location on Earth—**latitude** and **longitude**.

Imagine that Earth is a big ball. Latitude lines go around Earth horizontally. The **equator** is the line going around the middle of Earth. Lines north of the equator are positive numbers that go up from 0 to 90 to the North Pole. They are followed by an N for "north of the equator." Lines south of the equator are numbers from 0 to 90. They are followed by an S for "south of the equator." Lines of latitude tell how far north or south of the equator a place is.

▼ *What number would the equator be?*

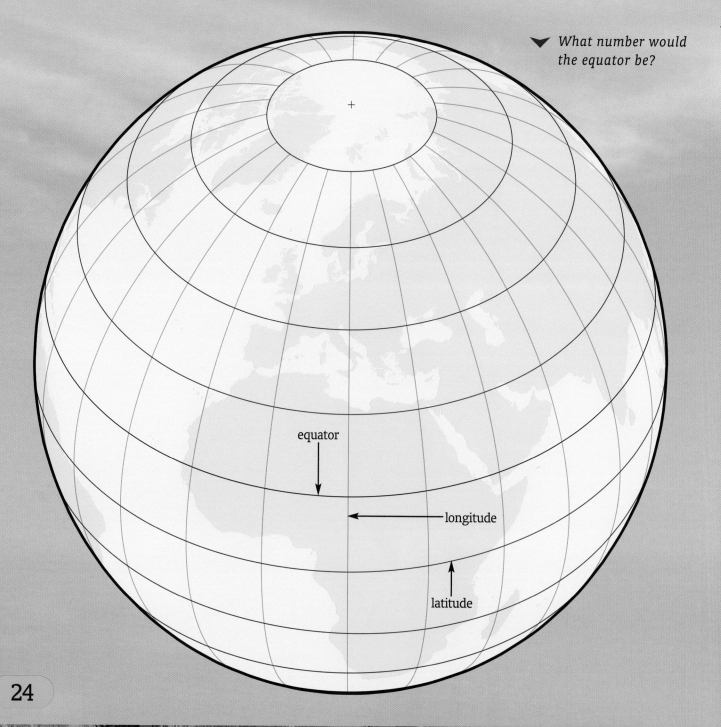

equator

longitude

latitude

A line from the North Pole to the South Pole is a line of longitude. Lines of longitude tell how far east or west a place is. Imagine that Earth is an orange. Longitude lines would cut the orange into sections.

Look at the globe and the map. Lines going from side-to-side are lines of latitude. Lines going up and down are lines of longitude. Look for them on other maps that you see!

Map Facts

The longitude line with a value of 0 is a line called the **prime meridian**. The line runs through Greenwich, England.

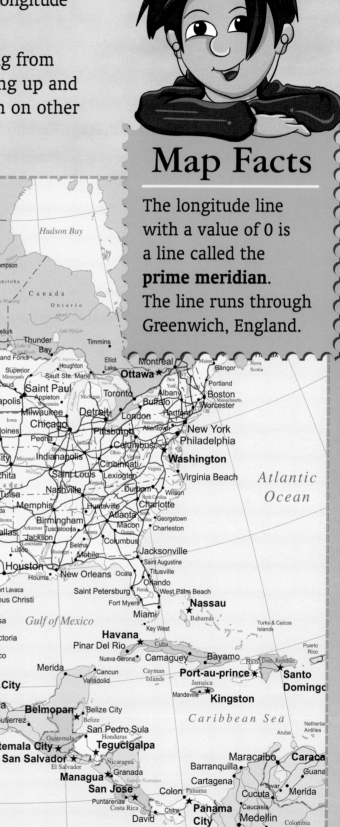

Scale and Distance

I drew a map from my house to one of my favorite places, Safeco Field!

How can you figure out the distance to travel between two places? Most maps have **scales**. A scale shows the relationship between the distance on the map and the distance on the ground. On some maps, for example, an inch (2.54 cm) could be the same as one mile (1.6 km). So if you measured one inch (2.54 cm) on the map, traveling that same distance on the ground would mean traveling one mile (1.6 km).

Qwest Field Event Center

Qwest Field Event Center Garage

4th Ave S

S Royal Brougham Way

Safeco Field

Alaskan Way Viaduct

Alaskan Way S

3 miles (1.6 km)

3rd Ave S

99

S Atlantic St

Colorado Ave S

Utah Ave S

1st Ave S

Occidental Ave

3rd Ave

26

The Seattle Mariners play baseball at Safeco Field. Look at my drawn map. I put an arrow from my house to the field and wrote the distance: 3 miles.

Now look at the map below. On this map, the scale tells you that one inch (2.54 cm) is the same as one mile (1.6 km). You could use a ruler to measure between points on a map. You would measure 3 inches (7.62 cm). That is the same as 3 miles (4.82 km).

▼ *Put your finger on the scale. It tells you that each inch (2.54 cm) on the map is one mile (1.6 km) on the street.*

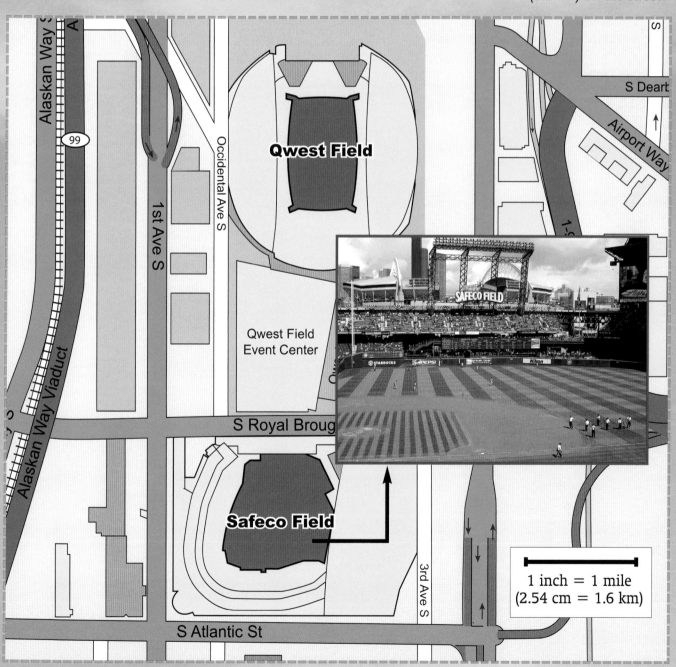

1 inch = 1 mile
(2.54 cm = 1.6 km)

A map can show a large scale or a small scale. A **large-scale map** shows an area that is small. On a large-scale map, one inch (2.54 cm) could represent one mile (1.6 km)—or even less! A **small-scale map** is the opposite. It shows an area that is relatively large. On a small-scale map, an inch (2.54 cm) could represent 1 mile (1.6 km), 100 miles (160.93 km), or even more!

This is a large-scale map of Safeco Field. It shows some of the streets that are near the stadium. The scale shows the distance measured in miles and kilometers.

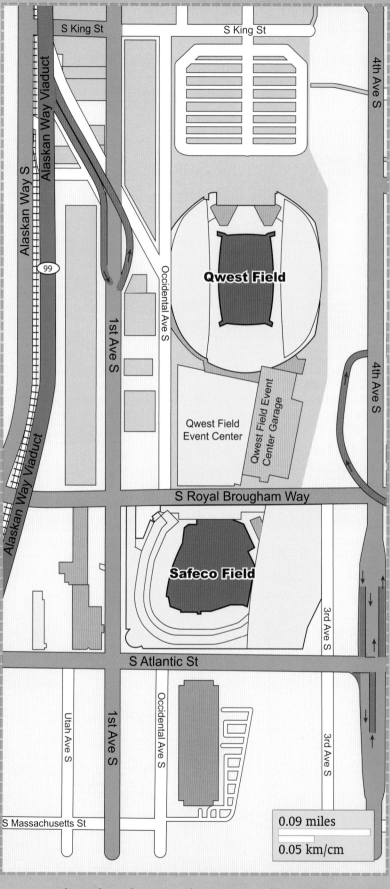

▲ *What places on this map would you like to visit?*

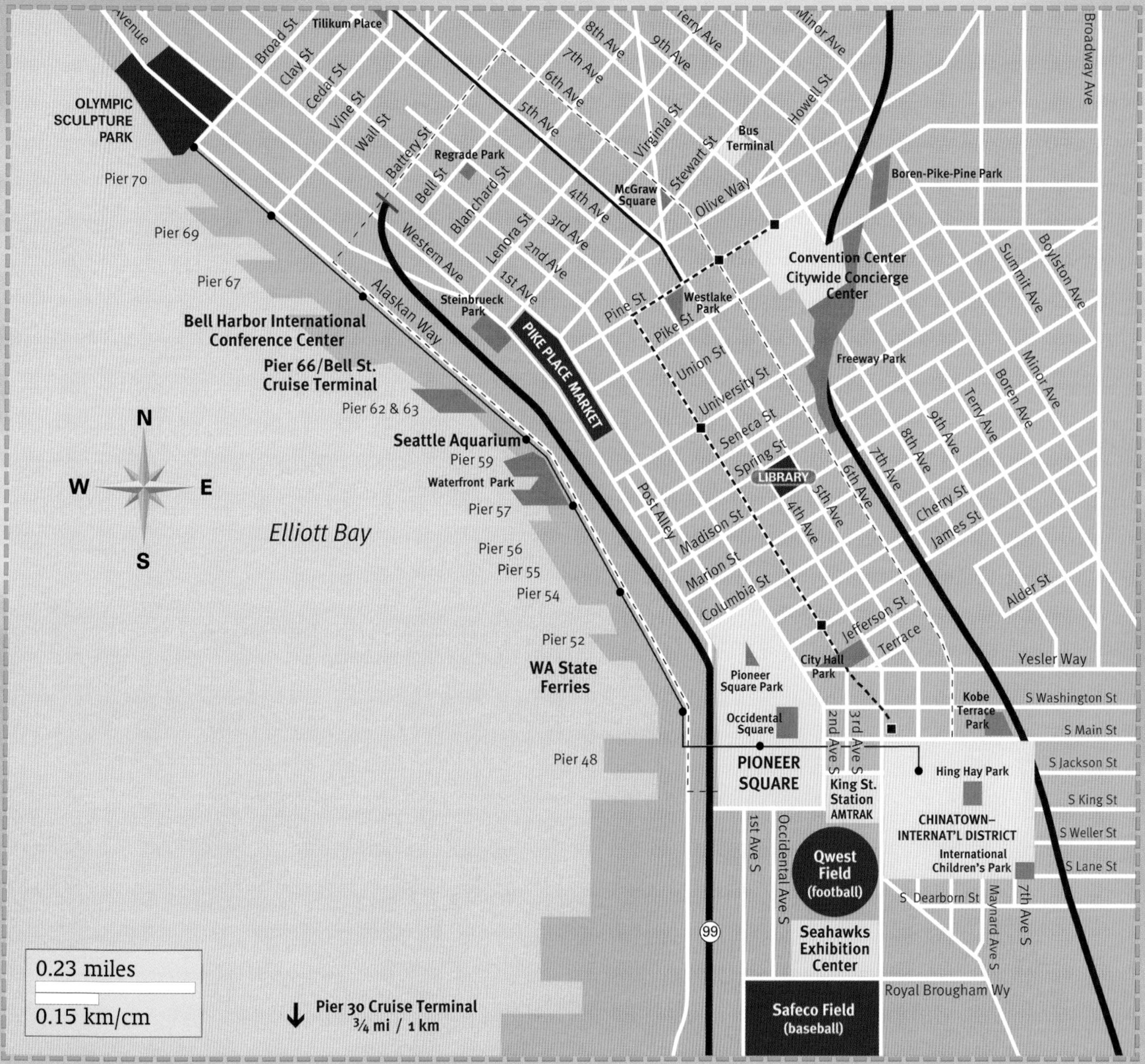
OLYMPIC SCULPTURE PARK
Pier 70
Pier 69
Pier 67
Bell Harbor International Conference Center
Pier 66/Bell St. Cruise Terminal
Pier 62 & 63
Seattle Aquarium
Pier 59
Waterfront Park
Pier 57
Pier 56
Pier 55
Pier 54
Pier 52
WA State Ferries
Pier 48
Elliott Bay
N
W
E
S
0.23 miles
0.15 km/cm
Pier 30 Cruise Terminal
3/4 mi / 1 km
Tilikum Place
Broad St
Clay St
Cedar St
Vine St
Wall St
Battery St
Bell St
Blanchard St
Lenora St
Regrade Park
Western Ave
Alaskan Way
1st Ave
2nd Ave
3rd Ave
4th Ave
5th Ave
6th Ave
7th Ave
8th Ave
9th Ave
Terry Ave
Minor Ave
Howell St
Virginia St
Stewart St
Bus Terminal
McGraw Square
Olive Way
Boren-Pike-Pine Park
Broadway Ave
Convention Center
Citywide Concierge Center
Steinbrueck Park
PIKE PLACE MARKET
Pine St
Pike St
Westlake Park
Union St
University St
Seneca St
Spring St
LIBRARY
Madison St
Marion St
Columbia St
Post Alley
Freeway Park
Summit Ave
Boylston Ave
Boren Ave
Cherry St
James St
Alder St
Jefferson St
Terrace
City Hall Park
Pioneer Square Park
Occidental Square
PIONEER SQUARE
Yesler Way
S Washington St
Kobe Terrace Park
S Main St
S Jackson St
Hing Hay Park
S King St
King St. Station AMTRAK
2nd Ave S
3rd Ave S
1st Ave S
Occidental Ave S
Qwest Field (football)
CHINATOWN– INTERNAT'L DISTRICT
International Children's Park
S Weller St
S Lane St
S Dearborn St
Maynard Ave S
7th Ave S
99
Seahawks Exhibition Center
Royal Brougham Wy
Safeco Field (baseball)

A small-scale map like this shows a larger land area.

This is a small-scale map. Safeco Field is smaller on the map! But now you can see more area than on a large-scale map.

Map Facts

Some maps use metric measurements such as meters. Some use standard measurements such as miles. Look carefully at the scale when you figure out distances.

What Do You Know About Reading Maps?

Imagine this: Your family is in Seattle, and you are all interested in visiting the aquarium. But you need to find it! Since you are the expert at reading maps, you know what to do. Describe how to get from Qwest Field to the aquarium. Use the compass rose, legend, and scale to describe the trip you will take.

▼ *This family reads a map to find their way to the aquarium.*

Is the aquarium in the eastern or western part of the city?

----------- Free Ride Area

——— Train Route

-------- Bus Tunnel

■ Bus Tunnel Stops

•——• Waterfront Street Car Route

■ Major Attractions

▪ Parks

▶ *Read the legend to help you find the aquarium.*

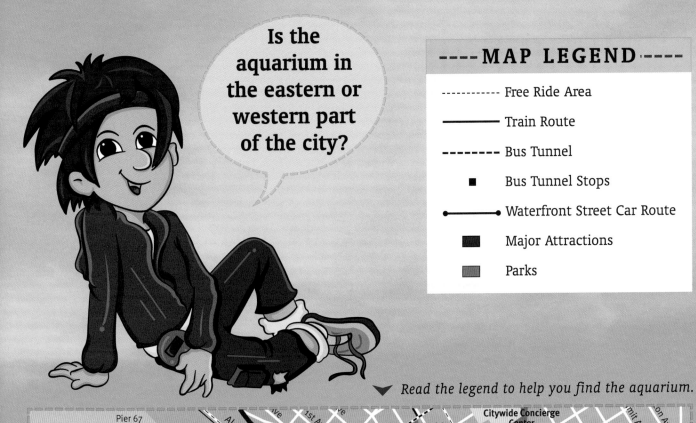

Pier 67

Alaskan Way

1st Ave

Steinbrueck Park

PIKE PLACE MARKET

Pine St

Pike St

Westlake Park

Citywide Concierge Center

Bell Harbor International Conference Center

Pier 66/Bell St. Cruise Terminal

Pier 62 & 63

Seattle Aquarium
Pier 59

Waterfront Park

Pier 57

Union St

University St

Seneca St

Spring St

Freeway Park

Post Alley

LIBRARY

4th Ave

5th Ave

6th Ave

7th Ave

8th Ave

9th Ave

Terry Ave

Boren Ave

Minor Ave

Elliott Bay

Pier 56

Pier 55

Pier 54

Madison St

Marion St

Columbia St

Cherry St

James St

Alder St

Pier 52

WA State Ferries

Jefferson St

Terrace

Yesler Way

N
W   E
S

Pioneer Square Park

City Hall Park

Occidental Square

Pier 48

PIONEER SQUARE

1st Ave S

Occidental Ave S

2nd Ave S

3rd Ave S

Kobe Terrace Park

S Washington S

S Main S

Hing Hay Park

S Jackson S

King St. Station AMTRAK

CHINATOWN– INTERNAT'L DISTRICT

S King S

S Weller S

Qwest Field (football)

International Children's Park

S Lane S

99

S Dearborn St

Maynard Ave S

7th Ave S

Seahawks Exhibition Center

Royal Brougham Wy

Safeco Field (baseball)

0.23 miles

0.15 km/cm

↓ Pier 30 Cruise Terminal
¾ mi / 1 km

31

Glossary

Note: Some boldfaced words are defined where they appear in the book.

compass rose A design on a map that shows direction

equator An imaginary circle around Earth between the north and south poles

Global Positioning System (GPS) A tool that tells your exact latitude and longitude

legend A small table that explains the map's symbols

latitude The distance north or south from the equator

longitude The distance east or west from the prime meridian

map A graphic representation of a place

scale The ratio between the distance on the map and the distance in the real world

symbol A picture that stands for something else

Index

compass rose 20, 21, 30

directions 20, 21, 22, 23, 24

equator 24

features
  made by people 12, 13, 14, 15
  natural 12, 13, 14, 15
  on maps 12, 13, 14

globe 11, 13, 25

GPS (Global Positioning System) 23

hiking trail 15

latitude 24, 25

legend 16, 17, 18, 19, 30, 31

longitude 24, 25

map-maker 16

Mount Rainier 14, 15, 16, 22, 23

prime meridian 25

relative location 22

scale 26–29, 30
  large scale map 28, 29
  small scale map 28, 29

street/road 5, 7, 9, 12, 13, 16, 18, 19, 27, 28

symbol 6, 16, 17, 18, 19, 20

Printed in the U.S.A. - CG